# The art of being imperfect: What do you have to be again?

Leo D. Dennis

Table of contents

# Chapter 1

## Being imperfect

This simply means you're not perfect. You don't have the perfect body, the perfect grades, the perfect personality, the perfect lifestyle, the perfect looks e.t.c. It means you make mistakes and that's perfectly fine and a good sign you're human. Of course, you can't be perfect. You might argue with me " oh, but I know someone who is"  but that person is perfect only to YOU and you can be perfect in someone's eyes too. Life is like that, no human is perfect all-round.

We all have our strengths and weaknesses. This brings us to accepting your imperfect self and fully embracing the true you and not who you think you should be at the moment.

## If you don't accept yourself then...who will?

If you tend to be more forgiving of others' faults than yours, you're probably too harsh on yourself. Some of you even bring yourselves down, you don't even need people to discourage you. I mean you just self-destruct, boom!
Know that those people aren't better than you. You were formed with a unique set of abilities that no one else possesses.

Plus, everyone makes mistakes! We're just human.
Becoming more tolerant of yourself and appreciating yourself for the excellent person that you are may lead you to greater happiness and more satisfying existence.

Here's how:

- **Focus on your excellent characteristics**

When you concentrate on becoming the greatest person you can be, you bring the finest possible life, love, and possibilities to you. It's only natural
Even though self-improvement is a desirable thing, you must recognize and concentrate on your positive traits, rather than focus on the attributes you feel poorly about.

Maintaining this positive perspective will not only help you better accept yourself, but it'll also make it simpler for you to reach your objectives by employing your strengths to propel yourself ahead.

- **Consciously inhibit negative thought processes**.

  This is essential to every single thing you want to actually put effort in and succeed. If you think positively, you'll see possibilities instead of roadblocks.

Negative thinking may snowball rapidly if you don't get ahead of it. It's alright to be in a foul mood every once in a while and have some unpleasant thoughts; it occurs to everyone.

The difficulty is in learning how to put those negative ideas aside and replace them with something pleasant. Replace your negative ideas about yourself with positives.Like affirmations.

Affirmations are positive remarks that confirm your great attributes and help bring out the best in you.

If you believe in yourself, you can accomplish basically anything. It's simply that easy.

- **Accept your imperfections**

It's not about concealing your shortcomings; it's about embracing them and being unapologetic about them.

Another element of being human is having certain faults.

Instead of concentrating on the things you can't alter, embrace them for what they are. Making the most of your life begins with embracing your shortcomings.

- **Use positive self-talk**

The way you choose to think and talk about yourself is your CHOICE. You may have spent your entire life negatively talking about yourself, but it doesn't mean you have to keep being pessimistic.

Positive self-talk may help you accomplish amazing things and transform the way you think about yourself.

Make it a necessity to provide real praises to yourself. I mean genuine ones.

Compliment yourself for the nice aspects of your appearance, your great attributes, and every time you accomplish anything properly.

Do this every day until it becomes a habit.

- **Disregard what other people may think about your choices.**

You shouldn't heed what others say about you. Let people compare you to whomever they want to, but you shouldn't even pay attention to them. Why? Because you don't even have time for such. You don't.

- **You'll never make everyone pleased.**

If you attempt to accomplish that, you'll quickly learn that, not only will other people still be miserable, but you'll also be fatigued and unhappy yourself. Trying to please everyone can simply be you looking for "validation" by making them happy but I assure you, you need no validation from anyone!

Make your own choices according to your priorities and be sure that you've done what is appropriate for you.

- **Avoid worrying**

There is a significant distinction between anxiety and concern. A worried person perceives a problem, and a concerned person fixes the issue.
Worrying will never assist your position, you surely know that.
Rather than wasting your time by being overwhelmed by worry, take action to do what you can to make the situation better.
If there's nothing you can do to alter it, concentrate on going ahead in other ways.
Try your best and realize that you've done all you could.

Let go of any negative ideas, such as being upset with yourself for not being able to perform an impossible accomplishment.
Even when you haven't done your best, find a way to make peace with yourself.
Move on and resolve to try harder next time.

**Note that:** What is behind us and what lies ahead of us are trivial things compared to what resides inside us.

In altering the way you think about yourself, you'll also change the way you perceive the world.
Every day brings up new chances for you, and by adopting positive thinking, you can make a genuine impact.

A lack of self-acceptance may hold you back in every aspect of your life. It impairs your confidence and might hinder you from attaining your full potential.
People with strong self-acceptance are more resilient to criticism. They recognize that it's appropriate to accept oneself while simultaneously striving for ongoing self-improvement.
Some individuals are more self-accepting than others. This can be related to variables like what the parents thought appropriate when they were younger and their childhood experiences.
As children, we tend to seek approval from our parents and some of us still do. So most times we conceal and evaluate other

portions of ourselves that were not accepted.

As an example, certain families deem some emotions acceptable and others not so much. Let's imagine you were up in a home where anger wasn't acceptable, you could find it difficult to express yourself when you feel furious. And this applies to certain other emotions too, including melancholy.
Here where I live, you are instructed not to weep even when you want to. And this is much more forced on boys. I realize you don't want your children crying every time they're angry or confront a difficulty. It's still not ethical to force youngsters to bottle up their sentiments. Well, that's my opinion..

So if your parents were extremely demanding, your inner voice could be highly critical and you might develop a fear of failing. This makes it tougher to accept oneself.

**What's your degree of self-acceptance?**
You may already know whether your degree of acceptance is high or low. One way to know is by looking back at your youth. Were your parents tough on you and not the behavior? If your response is yes, your self-acceptability is probably low.
Here are a few signs:

- Your view on life is merely gloomy for no reason at all.
- You tend to be unclear about your own identity.
- You have a deep yearning to be someone other than who you are.
- You have trouble communicating about your shortcomings

Know that genuine self-acceptance doesn't emerge overnight thus everyday practice and self-care assist you progressively. You'll eventually understand you don't need external affirmation. Accepting oneself immensely benefits your mental health.

# Chapter 2

## Why accepting oneself is crucial to self-love and self-respect

Self-acceptance is the antidote to self-judgment. If you judge yourself harshly and this leads to anxiety and sadness or other mental health difficulties, then it may be quite good to practice self-acceptance. With enough practice at self-acceptance, you can stop criticizing yourself and stop damaging yourself with the terrible effect of negative self-judgment.

**The Importance of Self Acceptance**
Things more essential than embracing yourself for who and what you are. You cannot increase your self-esteem without first knowing the necessity of

self-acceptance. Self-acceptance helps you to recognize and be honest about your strengths and faults. By embracing yourself, you open the door to self-care and a far more positive attitude towards who you are. This will provide the chance to grow and enhance yourself and your life.

**Self Acceptance Helps You Face Challenges**

When issues come up, as they definitely will, you need to be honest with yourself to overcome them. It is never a good idea to pretend to the world, and much worse to conceal the truth from yourself. It's not even conceivable to perform the second, even though many individuals strive to do precisely that.

Accepting the qualities about yourself that you cannot alter, such as your personality and character, is incredibly crucial as a beginning point in self-growth.

One additional wonderful thing about embracing who you are is that it might offer you a better and more accurate sense of your self-image. In other words, when you look at yourself, you will see more of the actual you and less will be concealed.

**Not Accepting Yourself Creates Inner Conflict**

The significance of self-acceptance is such that if you don't practice it, you may have some of the following problems:

- Poor self-esteem
  rejecting who you are or being oblivious to what you desire implies you may suffer from low self-esteem.

- Living a lie
  If you do not accept yourself and pretend to be what you are not, the outcome is a fake life. If you believe you are living a life that is not you,

possibly you have this issue. It needs solving.

- Unhappiness
  As a consequence of the foregoing, poor self-worth and living a lie will prohibit you from enjoying life, as you are neglecting your inner voice, your values, and the wishes of your heart.

- Becoming a victim
  Not accepting yourself makes it much easier to fall victim to people's negativity.

- Lacking self-belief
  Poor self-confidence might stem from being unclear about who you are and what you desire. This might also be made worse by your sentiments of being a victim.

**A word of warning**: occasionally, there are things we desire to forget about. What has occurred to us or what we have done. This is wonderful in concept but we must recognize the reality since circumstances no matter how horrific have made us what we are today. Never shut out the facts or reject them, it's better to be honest, particularly with yourself. If you battle with anything in your history or something you cannot manage, get assistance, and do not suffer alone.

**Self Acceptance makes you more honest with yourself**

Self-acceptance implies that you recognize who you genuinely are and where your strengths and shortcomings lie. You know what you want. This will help you to be content with your position in the world and be honest with yourself. Self-acceptance is one of the major qualities that help towards happiness in life.

This is incredibly significant for various reasons. The first is that if you know who you are, you may be more confident in that person. You may also be more real, rather than striving to be something different. This should help you feel comfortable in your skin and less worried.

Secondly, if you accept yourself, you may decide to be more honest about what you can do to utilize your skills to their greatest use. Which career would best fit you? What lifestyle do you long for? With self-acceptance, you can respect your decisions rather than trying to please others.

## Accepting Yourself Reduces Self Criticism

Another source of low self-esteem is negative self-talk. This is very critical and can hold a person back. Freeing ourselves from self-criticism, then begin to confront the obstacles in your life and conquer them.

Imagine being comfortable with others, being able to talk in public, and feeling good about yourself.
Acceptance Increases your self esteem. Self-acceptance helps you to view yourself from a better perspective.

If you accept yourself you also appreciate yourself. As a consequence, you will inform people that they should appreciate who you are. You will also be able to tolerate others and not insist that they attempt to attain your expectations. You will also be able to ask people for what you want and need. Accepting oneself will help you to stop warring in your head. You may resolve conflict within yourself by just being honest about who you truly are.

Self-acceptance indicates that you are pleased with yourself and what you are, but it does not imply that you give up hope of change or progress. Self-acceptance, as I describe here, can help you make

substantial progress in your self-development because you need to realize the truth about yourself. You may then accept it and determine whether or not you can change.
Self-acceptance does not entail being pleased with your existing circumstances or remaining still. Rather, you are free to alter what you can in total honesty with your reality.

What measures can you take to boost your self-acceptance?
We have covered the necessity of self-acceptance, but how do you go about embracing yourself? Here are several measures you may take:

Take time to reflect on who you are, your personality, your past, what makes you tick. Understand that there are both great and bad parts of who you are and you should accept them if you cannot alter them. Denying the truth benefits no one.

Are there aspects about yourself that you don't like? OK, maybe you can improve but first, admit them and accept them.
Are you pretending to be something you're not? Why are you doing this? Wouldn't it be better, to be honest with yourself?

## These mindsets eat up your personal satisfaction

- **Everyone assesses you**

No, they don't. You simply feel that way either because you're anxious about a certain thing, maybe you dress a little bit differently than you normally do, or your hairdo isn't as dull as other people's, or maybe you think your make-up has miraculously changed to a clown's.
Maybe you feel uneasy in public, you could believe you're walking strange or something but it's all in your brain. Really.
Even if they're truly staring, simply take a big breath and say" I don't care". Problem solved.
It's not that simple, I know but try it.

- **Your loved ones will be unhappy if you're not perfect**

Dude, what! Well, this varies from family to family however, if your family loves you they can't be dissatisfied since no human is flawless. They can't expect you to be flawless since they are not themselves. If you have loved ones or parents who want you to be flawless at everything, you probably shouldn't listen to what they have to say every time. You could feel this way maybe because your parents are quite rigid. Maybe they don't support you or they criticize you every time they get. If your loved ones are like this… yes they're toxic I'm sorry. So do not take everything they say to heart, think about how far you've come. You are your person.

- **You have to be better than everyone else**

It's wonderful to aim to be the greatest in everything you do, but you should always be your competition.
Using your prior success as a starting point to where you want to go, and what you want

to do makes you better every time at what you do.
When you start striving to be better than every single person, you go all over the place and don't get one thing done.
Doing this, envy and comparison emerge from it. You think "wow this individual is doing a lot better than I am" and you start feeling inferior. Don't. You have your distinct talents, you have what you can do and you have to realize that there are certain things you cannot perform at a given moment. Yes, you have a lot to learn and you can always gain ideas from a person you believe is above you and keep growing at your own pace. With consistency, you realize you're already doing better than you ever anticipated.
We all compare other people's life to ours. It's only human nature to aspire to be better, do better, be the greatest but when it's too much, it's too much.
So don't purposefully have it in mind to be better than a person by all means since you

risk harming your growth. So I think if you should constantly take your prior successes as a starting point. You grow better every single time.

# Chapter 3

## 1. Acknowledge your shortcomings

When you learn to embrace your shortcomings, you learn how to be content with who you are now until you get to where you want to be. You don't compare yourself to others ahead of you and feel uneasy about yourself and your successes.

You don't look at accepting your defects as complacency or lack of ambition, you look at it as compassion and self-love; knowing you'll never be flawless, you'll never look a particular way and you'll never totally appreciate everything about yourself but it won't stop you from loving your imperfections. Learning to embrace what you can't change. Feeling good enough and understanding your value instead than looking at yourself from the perspective of others.

When you learn to accept your shortcomings, you're less subject to people's judgments, remarks, or views about you. No one can disgrace you or hold them against you. You accept the idea that you're human and you're learning and you still have a long way to go.
The advantage of learning to embrace your shortcomings is that it takes away the need to impress others or constantly try to measure up to someone.

When you learn to accept your shortcomings you attract individuals who accept them too. You discover people that don't make you feel like you need to alter who you are. You discover folks that enjoy the fact that you're a bit quirky, a little unusual, a little sloppy, a little bizarre but they love you anyways!

When you learn to accept your flaws, instead of making them bigger issues, create a healthier environment for yourself. You become more emotionally intelligent.

- **Find the good side in your weaknesses**

The first step towards accepting faults is to be conscious and adjust your viewpoint about how you see yourself. Stop perceiving yourself as deficient or lacking in particular areas, and start seeing yourself as a full person, however imperfect. Moreover, upon contemplation, you may realize that your defects or shortcomings provide you with a distinct advantage.

For example, my fixation with creating a thoroughly researched work made me aware of my inclination to postpone if I don't find the final written work to be up to my expectations. Learning to perceive your weaknesses as your strengths might be a long process, but you'll be able to see yourself from a better perspective through establishing self-validation.

### 2. Realize that your faults make you human

Imperfections give you character and make you real. Whenever you find yourself becoming persuaded again by the image of someone who's wonderfully put-together and efficient, try envisioning that person in your everyday existence. You may be astonished by the realization that their flawlessness can begin to bother or weary you in no time.

Most of us strive to erase our oddities and conceal eccentricities rather than embrace them as a key part of our identities in the pursuit of perfection. In truth, your impression of being flawed or defective may be arising from self-perception that may emphasize just one part of your personality.

Indeed, you may be entirely uninformed of how your so-called defects may bring a feeling of completeness to your image in the eyes of others.

**3. Focus on flow state instead than perfection**

We sometimes incorrectly feel that perfection is a precondition for the completion of objectives. Indeed, objectives help us go ahead, but they shouldn't function as roadblocks that remind us of what we lack.

**4. Use your shortcomings to assist others**

The world breaks everyone and thereafter many become stronger.

Once you recognize that throwing your concerns aside and embracing your genuine self makes you honest, you may assist others to grasp this as well. Reveling in your weaknesses and continuing to put your best effort forward by accepting defects might encourage countless people who feel hampered by their shortcomings.

It's crucial to remember that your faults and defects make you genuine. Indeed, some of these imperfections you may be able to repair to realize your goal or to progress into a better version of yourself, while other deficiencies are destined to be a part of you forever. Embracing faults is crucial to having a genuine and fulfilled life.

"You're doing great"

Leo

www.ingramcontent.com/pod-product-compliance
Lightning Source LLC
LaVergne TN
LVHW052113160826
845678LV00015B/3534

* 9 7 9 8 3 5 2 7 4 3 7 4 4 *